NAMED

THE WOMEN

A WORKBOOK FOR INDIVIDUALS AND SMALL GROUPS

Contributors for *Named: The Women* include Annie Carter, Erina Ludwig, Julie Joiner, and Katie Savage.

CONTENTS

INTRODUCTION

Noah, The Woman at the Well, Thomas, Hagar; these men and women are more than just names in Bible stories. They were flesh and blood people. And in seeing how God moved in their lives, we can see him moving in ours. We can hear him call us by name.

Named is a 6-week small group resource that tells the story of people from scripture through a new lens—exploring the mystery of faith with a literary touch. Each series introduces 6 different people from the Bible, unpacking one person's story every week.

This workbook has original stories that are accompanied by historical context for the characters and the times they lived in, insight into how they fit into God's story, and discussion questions to help participants see how God's story works in them. This is a unique opportunity for your group to engage the Scriptures both personally, and as a community. Through the power of history-based stories, you'll see the truth of how God works. Not just in ancient times and in other people, but how he works today and in us all. Become acquainted with the people identified by God in a story as particular as yours.

HOW TO GET THE MOST OUT OF THIS STUDY

This workbook sheds light on six women touched by God in unique ways. In a time where females had little value in the world, God used these individuals to protect, serve, love and lead in ways that impacted generations to come.

The narratives are written to help you to begin to think about how these individuals might have been feeling or what they might have been thinking during their story. Each week before you get together with your group, you might want to read the scriptures that the narrative is based on so that you have a full picture of the story. As you work through the reading and journaling in this book, continue to think about the pieces of the stories that find themselves in your life. What can you learn from these stories and apply in your own life?

WHAT YOU'LL FIND IN EACH CHAPTER

CONTEXT

This section will give readers an understanding of what was going on around the person at the time of the story. Historical, societal, and religious background are given to help readers put themselves in the shoes of those whose stories they are about to read.

STORY

The narratives told in this study attempt to get inside the heads of those whose stories we may have heard hundreds of times before. The writers of these pieces have attempted, through research and reflection, to give us a brief glimpse into what these people might have been thinking and how they might have felt. As you read or listen to the story each week look for places where you can relate to the story—God's story.

PLACE IN GOD'S STORY

This section will give you a short description of how God's story found its place in this individual.

THE STORY FINDS ITS PLACE IN ME

These questions are designed to help you reflect on what you've read in order to find yourself in God's narrative. There is plenty of space available for journaling.

WRITERS

Annie Carter grew up in Oklahoma with her parents and two older sisters. She holds a BS in communications and creative writing from Olivet Nazarene University in Kankakee, Illinois. Annie has been a student at The Writers Studio in New York since April of 2012. She currently lives in New York City with her cat, Olive.

Erina Ludwig is the author of *Unnoticed Neighbors: A Pilgrimage into the Social Justice Story* and writes for the *Indy Star, Indy Spectator,* and *Pattern Magazine.* She holds a history degree from King's College London and was chosen to be one of six European journalists to tour and discuss youth political apathy across the States in 2004 by the U.S. Foreign Press Center. Currently, she is working on her own work of young adult fiction. A Londoner at heart, she now lives in Indianapolis with her husband and their excitable puppy, Lucy.

Julie Joiner invested more than eight years writing and editing Sunday School curriculum for Nazarene Publishing House. She earned her BA in writing and literature from Burlington College and MA in counseling from MidAmerica Nazarene University. The roles in which she ministers are intern counselor for New Vision Counseling Center; writer; mom of two grown daughters; and wife of Jim, a man of ministry.

Katie Savage is the author of *Grace in the Maybe: Instructions on Not Knowing Everything About God.* She has a BA in English Education and Creative Writing from Point Loma Nazarene University and an MFA from the University of Kansas. She and her husband Scott live in Kansas City with their two children.

HAGAR

THE STRANGER • KEY SCRIPTURE PASSAGES:

Genesis 16, 21

HER CONTEXT

Sarah and Hagar represent two different social classes. Sarah was the wife of Abraham, who was the recipient of the divine promises. She was the matriarch in the family. She had the power to control the destiny of those who served her. Even her husband listened to her. Hagar was a slave, a foreigner, an Egyptian, unrelated to the Amorite group of Sarah. She stood outside the divine promises. So Sarah represents the powerful element in the society; Hagar represents the poor and the afflicted. Sarah, however, lacked something very important to an ancient woman; She was not a mother. Though she was Abraham's wife, she had borne him no children.

> "Hagar was a slave, a foreigner, an Egyptian, unrelated to the Amorite group of Sarah. She stood outside the divine promises."

According to the ancient thinking, barrenness was a divine curse. The ancient social customs provided a legal process through which a barren woman could remove this shame. In the event of barrenness a wife could give her personal maid to her husband. Children born out of this relationship legally became the children of the wife. Hagar was introduced here as Sarah's hope, a person who could remove her shame. In addition, Hagar became Abraham's wife through this Amorite custom. His relationship with Hagar was a legal act in this culture, and Hagar's status was now elevated, making Sarah's rejection of her highly irregular for that time.

HER STORY

It was stifling under the canvas tent in the wake of hours of exertion. The woman was still in the middle of the floor, shivering with the shallow in and out of pained breaths.

To the woman's left, shadowed in the artificial darkness of the small tent, stood a man. He was called Abraham by his neighbors. The man was built of strong shoulders, even if sunk slightly with age. He stood with his arms crossed over his chest looking at the woman he'd taken to bed eight and a half months ago. He turned his head away. His back ached. A back that felt a weight he did not yet understand. He put his hand to his neck and rubbed hard into the knots across his shoulders. He was tired and wondered where his wife was and why she had not come to the tent with him. Then he turned and just stood watching the woman.

She was sinking to the floor. The pain was so great that she lost her breath. Her head lolled over her right shoulder and rested against the forearm of the young nurse. The round midwife below her stood and took an apple from a wicker basket on the floor and pulled a small sharp knife from the folds of cloth tied like an apron around her waist, and then she balanced the apple on the floor and split it in half with one heavy cut of the blade. The black and shining seeds spilled from the core and scattered across the sandy ground away from the woman. The midwife held up half of the apple and pressed the wet spongy surface to the woman's nose.

The sour scent filled the enclosed space, and one of the nurses chanted a string of prayers, but the woman revived only a little. A short table beside her was strewn with jars and glass bottles filled with golden-colored oils and steaming water and wine. One small dish of olive oil had been toppled in the struggle of the delivery, and a greasy rivulet trailed from the tabletop down the wooden leg and across the floor but collected dust as it moved and congealed before ever reaching the woman's feet. The midwife wrung out a square of wool from a bowl of warm water and pressed the fomentation to the woman's forehead. The woman's Egyptian features shone strangely green with the loss of blood. Her head tilted loosely forward, and the dripping wool fell to her lap. Abraham did not go to her.

"Hagar."

He spoke her name. All three midwives turned their faces to him and paused together. A bleeding tableau. But the woman did not lift her head. He spoke to her again.

"Hagar."

After a breath, Hagar raised her chin from her chest and slowly turned to look at him in defiance of her anemic limbs. Sweat beaded under her nose and across her eyelashes, wetting the black kohl painted around them and leaving sooty gray streaks down her sallow face. She looked up at him, weary and compliant as a tethered ram eyeing her executioner with a wretched resignation to her own absurd sacrifice. Neither of them moved. They stared at one another in the darkness, and in that moment between them, the baby dropped silently from the woman into the hands of the crouching midwife. In the instant the child emptied its mother's womb, a flash passed over her eyes, and like a spell being broken, all faces in the room turned to see that the child was a boy.

The woman leaned back slowly until she rested against a tapestry pillow set on the floor behind her. She watched the boy writhe. The midwife cut the cord with the blade and laid a heavy sheepskin across the woman's lap. The nurses let go of her arms and busied themselves with the child. One broke the top from a sealed clay bottle and poured wine out onto the baby. It spread over his piqued face and down his back, and the nurse wet a square of wool and rubbed him down all over. He had been born with a full head of hair. Matted and black, with a thin line of it continuing down the nape of his neck and between his shoulder blades like a newly pulled kid goat. The midwife unwound a band of swaddling linen and began to bind the boy from his feet all the way up and around his shoulders. The child did not cry. The midwife cleaned her hands across her thighs and handed the tightly wrapped baby to Hagar and looked at them a moment and then turned away to blow out a small candle burning in a shallow ivory dish and left the tent.

The room emptied so quickly that Hagar was startled to find she was alone with Abraham. He crossed the floor and knelt in front of her. She could not bring herself to smile. He looked down at the child, and she couldn't tell what he was thinking or even if she cared. After a moment, and without a word, he got up to leave.

"His name," she started and then paused to make sure she had his attention, "is Ishmael."

Abraham looked at her face. She did not look away. He touched the boy's forehead and nodded. Then he wiped his hands on his shirtsleeves and turned from her and went to the curtain at the front of the tent and rent it aside. A shocking brake of midday sunlight made him wince. Age now showed in the deep creases around his eyes and his coarse white beard and the calluses across his hands. Rain was coming. He lifted his hand to shield his eyes from the sun and looked out across the sandy plain to the horizon. A smattering of livestock stood in the distance. Sprawling acres of land lay untouched and left vulnerable by men who had not learned to build fences or by no men at all.

A festoon of flowers and yew branches had been hung over the entry to the tent and now dangled strangely askew, dipping to the sand. Abraham studied it where it looked to have been torn away from the canvas. A young ibis stood under it, pulling the petals off of a blue crocus with its beak. A shadow moved over the bird, and it jumped and flew away. The man looked up. His wife stood between his face and the sun. She was barefoot in the sand. Her right hand was clenched in a fist around crumpled leaves from the damaged wreath. Abraham looked from the branches of the wreath to his wife's hands and then looked at her face. It was streaked with old tears cried hours ago. He asked her how she could be angry, and she laughed. —AC

"She looked up at him, weary and compliant as a tethered ram, eyeing her executioner with a wretched resignation to her own absurd sacrifice."

HER PLACE IN GOD'S STORY

Hagar's prominence in history began with her role as mother to Abraham's firstborn son. The name Hagar means "the stranger," a fitting descriptor for a woman who remained always outside of Abraham's elect tribe and outside of the given promise. And while in the Judeo-Christian tradition Hagar's portion of the story reads like an embarrassing mistake, a hiccup to an otherwise faithful story line, there is something to be said about the way God both sees and considers her humanity. In this way, he assigns a prophetic sense of worth upon those who are outsiders.

Before the birth of her son, God meets Hagar in the wilderness when her role as slave woman and concubine to Abraham has incited jealousy or put her at odds with Sarah. In Genesis 16, Hagar has just fled the camp in an attempt to escape from Sarah's harsh treatment when an angel of the Lord finds her by a spring of water (an important detail to note). "Behold, you are with child, and you will bear a son; and you shall call his name Ishmael, because the LORD has given heed to your affliction" (v. 11, NASB). In response, she calls upon the name of the Lord saying, "You are a God who sees" (v. 13, NASB).

Instructed to return, it isn't until many years later that a final departure takes place and Hagar and her son are forever sent away from the tribe and into the desert. As she was nearly dying of thirst, God reiterates his intentions for her line, "'Arise and lift up the lad, and hold him by the hand, for I will make a great nation of him.' Then God opened her eyes and she saw a well of water" (21:18-19, NASB).

The offering of water is significant. Not only was Hagar's thirst quenched and her life spared, but there is also a greater symbolism at play. Fast-forward. In the New Testament we read about another well scene. This one involved Christ and a Samaritan woman—a Gentile considered an outsider and stranger to the promise. How did

Christ treat the woman? He offered her himself—*the* living Water. The parallels are such that we can almost imagine Jesus speaking to Hagar herself rather than the Samaritan when he says, "Everyone who drinks of this water will thirst again; but whoever drinks of the water that I will give him shall never thirst" (John 4:13-14, NASB).

Christ, the Blessing, is for the chosen and the stranger alike.

THE STORY FINDS ITS PLACE IN ME

1. What elements of Hagar's story find their place in you?

HAGAR

2. Hagar was rejected by those she lived her life with. However, God valued her and had a plan for her. Tell of a time in your life when you felt rejected or outcast and God provided for you.

3. Hagar tried to leave. She'd given up on her seemingly hopeless situation, yet God called her back. What situation in your life is God asking you to come back to or stay in, relying on his grace to be sufficient?

4. Why do you think God chose the symbol of water to communicate the gift of himself—his acceptance and care to Hagar? What might be a symbol God would use today, in your life?

5. Though we hear little more of Hagar and Ishmael's story, we know that Hagar and Abraham birthed a nation through Ishmael. What does this tell us about how God views the stranger, the outcast, the broken?

NOTES

MIRIAM

THE IMPETUOUS • KEY SCRIPTURE PASSAGE: Numbers 12:1-15

HER CONTEXT

Miriam's Israel was one of a once-enslaved people, freedom, sea miracles, desert wanderings, and the long refrain of the Promised Land. Hers is the Israel we know of because of Moses, Ramses and a series of destructive plagues.

It is thought that the Israelites were enslaved for around 430 years. (Exod. 12:40) In some places it is written that Miriam was born in the earlier part of this harsh oppression of Israel, hence her name, which means 'sea of bitterness.' She would have been familiar with her place in such society. Where newborn Hebrew boys were thrown to crocodiles in the Nile to control the population. However, unlike others, she would have some reason to hope.

> "Miriam was born in the earlier part of this harsh oppression of Israel, hence her name, which means 'sea of bitterness.'"

Throughout hers and Israel's story in Exodus, Miriam is connected with water. At the start, she goes with her mother Jochebed to set Moses on the River Nile in his reed basket. At the crossing through of the Red Sea, it is Miriam who leads the women with a timbrel (a rhythm instrument), dance and song of praise that has been recorded and kept. This song preceded Deborah's battle cry by generations, but still had the same essence. It rallied people and reminded them of their God. It was about testimony, devotion and worship. It was probably not solely for their time, but for those to come, to know what had happened. Finally, after Miriam dies in Kadesh, springs of water with oases appear as they travel, but only after they dry up first (Exod. 20:1-11). This has led some to the 'cup of Miriam,' which is set upon the table at Passover Seder to remind all of her well.

The Israelites experienced many miracles during this time. They ate Manna, saw God as a pillar of cloud and fire and drank water in a dead desert. For hundreds of years Jewish people have attributed this to Moses, Aaron and Miriam. The Talmud even talks of how fish was added the Passover Seder to represent Leviathan and water, thus honoring Miriam.

HER STORY

The trouble with deserts is that you lose track of what day it is when you are in them. At first I knew. I used to count every day of our freedom. I knew how many days it had been since we had finally left the stones and marble of Pharaoh, but now time has faded. Each day bleeds into the other at a slow, tired pace—much like all of us.

We move along in our family groups, but the women stay with the children whilst some men take the front and others the rear. All around me are the sounds of animals braying, people bargaining over clothes and sandals and the gentle vibration of thousands of feet falling one after another.

The sound is so familiar; I have to check around for chariots and running hooves.

I spot Moses ahead. Even now as we march along there are so many gathered around him like birds and bees to flowers. His face is still and his eyes betray nothing. His beard is long and moon white and falls all the way down his chest. He leans more on his staff nowadays, and I see my brother has become old.

I see the round, soft-skinned babe, our mother held all those years ago. In my mind I can touch the woven basket that mother made with the Nile's reeds. I watch as those same reeds and the waters carry him off, so softly he slept the entire way.

It was our mother and how she sounds when she cries that made me wade a little closer to the princess and her attendants. They pulled back at first, but she listened when I spoke about a wet nurse. But it was Moses' face she was looking at.

The years slowed after that until, without seeing, it was the night death came to Egypt and took all the first born. On especially quiet nights I can still hear the cries. Not just mothers, but fathers too. I hear horns; doors opening and slamming, running feet and I hear the silence in our slave quarters.

Perhaps that was the first time I really felt the Egyptians might have been human too. That and when they were hurrying after us on the rocky base of the Red Sea. The wind had howled as heavily as the sea sprayed us.

I could see their armor, their swords and I knew it was because of their firstborn dead they had followed us to bury us too.

You would think a falling wall of water would make anyone nearby deaf, but this sea did not. It tipped and slipped and then raced down to the base rushing to cover them and their chariots. I can see Moses' face on the waters looking for his former kin. I think that is when he started to go gray.

Of course we sang to God. I shouted the loudest until I wasn't able to speak for the next few weeks. I danced and clapped. We were free. I was born a slave, but now we were free.

I turn to my left and see old Abel and Sara on a cart that one of Reuben's boys had made for them. Their pale gray donkey pulls them along. They have wandered with us in this deathly land and still we are no closer. We left Egypt with the promise of freedom and a place to call our own home and now we are vagrants.

I look and see Moses is still surrounded, but this time a dark brown-skinned woman draws near to him. He holds her hand and kisses it and something in me tears. Something starts to burn and it's catching.

"Whoever is on the receiving end of that look should find memorial stones right now."

I turn and see Aaron. He's leaner, but really just a slightly older version of Moses. I am surprised he is not up at the front with Moses, but I'm distracted.

"She isn't one of us. God made the promise to us," I say, harshly.

"Well according to our brother that promise turned into wandering about," says Aaron. His eyes narrow and his mouth is a grim line.

I find I am walking now. I am walking faster than I have for a while. I hear Aaron call me. He's shuffling. He cannot walk as fast.

The men around Moses are pleading for this and bartering for that. I try and slip between them, but they part anyway. I am his sister.

"Miriam," he says. He smiles for the first time all day. The woman behind him has a faltering smile. She can read me already.

"You were wrong to bring her here among us. How could you have married a Cushite?" The word comes out like a hiss.

"Miriam . . ." he starts to say. The smile is gone now.

"No, Moses. Do not quarrel with your sister," She says softly.

"You're supposed to be our leader, but instead you've led us into nothingness," I continue.

"Surely you're not God's only servant?" Aaron has joined us. None of us realize we have stopped walking and so have the rest. Except they keep a distance from us.

I expect Moses to throw his staff down and tear his robe, but instead he holds it tighter with both hands. His shoulders sag and then we see the tears. They wet his cheeks and stain his robe.

"Have mercy. Please have mercy," he whispers, but desperately.

At first I think he means us and then I see what he is hiding his lowered face from—a pillar of cloud.

* * *

I have been in this little tent room for a week today. I look down my arms to my fingertips and see the dried white skin has shed and gone. If it's possible, my own skin looks younger.

After spending the week trying to forget the sound of God's voice, I think I finally achieve it.

I can still hear Moses and see him on his knees, face down, pleading and weeping loudly. Or perhaps it's loud because Aaron is there too. He can't kneel or his joints would lock.

We had all heard of skin illnesses, but to wear it on your own body, to feel yourself decay, the smell, the touch and the look of it. I didn't think seven days would be enough to get rid of it.

They had waited for me to heal, everyone, even the Cushite. They all set up camp and mourned my lost skin and punishment too.

Now as the sun rises on this seventh morning my tent door is pulled open.

He is quiet, only the gentle tapping of his staff breaking the peace. He sits beside me and takes my hand.

I try to apologize, but only cracking sounds come out the back of my throat. My hair is matted and I smell odd. I try again, but he stops me.

He shakes his head, his green-gray eyes watching me from under white eyebrows.

"There's no need. The penance has been paid." —EL

"Of course we sang to God. I shouted the loudest until I wasn't able to speak for the next few weeks. . . . We were free. I was born a slave, but now we were free."

HER PLACE IN GOD'S STORY

In both the Christian and Jewish traditions, Miriam has always been one of the celebrated matriarchs. Hers is a story we are familiar with. We may have wondered at her absences for large stretches of time in the Torah and Bible, but when she does appear, she is a pivotal player.

Miriam may have been the elder sister of a famed brother, but it was her daring spirit and trust in God that allowed Moses the opportunity to live. At a time when Pharaoh's death sentence on all Hebrew boys would have borne heavy punishments for those who defied it, she shows courage and reverence for life. (Exod. 2:1-4)

For some it may have been enough to see that Moses' basket docked safely with Pharaoh's daughter, but not Miriam. She goes further and talks directly to Egyptian royalty and manages to convince the princess to allow Moses' own birth mother, Jochebed to be his nurse. Her quick thinking and boldness allowed her mother more time with the son she was probably quite convinced she would never see again. (Exod. 2:7-9)

That said Miriam's outspokenness has also acted as a warning to God's people. When both she and Aaron criticize Moses on his Cushite bride and his own importance, she is punished with leprosy. Despite Moses' intercession, Miriam still had to endure the seven days wait for purification outside of the camp, which would eventually become law in dealing with skin diseases. (Num. 12:1- 15) (Deut. 24:8-9)

Miriam is the first person named in the Bible to be called prophet. Although scholars may dispute its actual terms in (Exod. 15:20-21), the rest of the Bible shows us what and who a prophet was.

THE STORY FINDS ITS PLACE IN ME

1. What parts of Miriam's story find their place in you?

2. Miriam lives through enslavement, escape and wandering in a desert. She does not live to see the Promised Land, but remains with her community. She shows us that value, riches and identity do not depend on our circumstances, but rather what we believe in. How have you been challenged in your beliefs?

3. Sometimes our biggest struggles can be with our own ideas about ourselves. Miriam was a prophet, yet she still raged against her brother for being "God's chosen." Have you found yourself comparing your importance against those close to you?

4. When Israel walks through the Red Sea, Miriam gets a tambourine and dances. She leads the other women into worship and sings loudly about what God has achieved. She seems very proud of God's work and is happy to share so. We all have different way of expressing worship—how have you chosen to do so?

5. Miriam's criticism of Moses' Cushite wife shows her human imperfection. Her attitude is addressed and Moses still comes to his sister's defense. Through this we see that divisions are something we can all work through. How can you take this into your life to work to get past the problems our human imperfection create?

NOTES

RUTH

THE REDEEMED • KEY SCRIPTURE PASSAGE: Ruth 1:16-17, 2-3

HER CONTEXT

The time between the conquest of Canaan and the anointing of Saul as the first king of Israel was the period of the Judges. This was a dark time in Israel's history, a time of total disregard towards the law of God. Israel gave themselves to doing whatever they pleased, only to return over and over again to plead with God to rescue them from the consequences of their sin. In the midst of this darkness God placed the story of Ruth, a laser light of redemption and hope. And God's redeemed was a woman from Moab, a culture revolving around evil practices which included sacrificing their babies to false gods. The Israelites hated the Moabites.

"The story of Ruth and Boaz is a story of redemption and foreshadows the fulfillment of complete redemption for all mankind through Christ Jesus."

The provision for a widow left without a son was made in Deuteronomy 25:5-10; the deceased husband's brother was to marry her. The redemption of property lost due to debt was addressed in Numbers 27:8-11; it was the duty of a near relative meeting the requirements of guardian-redeemer to redeem the land and keep it in the family. There was a closer kinsman to Ruth than Boaz, but he refused to take the responsibility of kinsman-redeemer. Boaz met the requirements for kinsman-redeemer: a close male relative, he had the financial means to redeem the land and he had a desire to be kinsman-redeemer for Ruth.

The story of Ruth and Boaz is a story of redemption and foreshadows the fulfillment of complete redemption for all mankind through Christ Jesus. Jesus, God's Son fulfilled the requirements to be our Redeemer: He became the Son of Man, He had the perfect blood to be the sacrifice for our sins and He gave himself willingly in obedience to God.

HER STORY

We came here widows destitute and grieving. She had announced, "I am going back to my homeland, Judah." Though she tried to turn me away, I clung to her and I followed her into a world foreign to me. The decision to go with Naomi led up to this moment, this night. From a detested people I came here with nothing but loyalty and a strong back from which to serve; I gathered grain as a beggar in one man's field. Great courage is required of me tonight as I tip-toe across his threshing floor in the dark.

Just hours ago my skin glistened under a slim ray of sunlight pushing through a crack in the door, still damp from soaking and scrubbing myself in anticipation of offering myself to Boaz. I reached for my tunic and pulled it on over my head. Nervousness moved down through my body and into my fingertips leaving them jittery. Naomi came in and found me struggling to tie the sash of my cloak.

"Daughter, let me help you." Her murmurings soothed me for the moment. "You look beautiful. Stay calm, child. God, our provider, will not fail you now. It is good for you to have a kinsman redeemer, a husband to return all you have lost."

This idea formed in Noami's mind over time as I described to her Boaz's kindness towards me. He had provided protection for me and an abundance of grain from which to glean; she hoped now he would provide a home.

How quickly the evening picked me up and delivered me to the threshing floor. Pinned down in a shadow just shy of the light, voices of men unaware come out to greet me. Laughter follows on the heels of jesting, "Boaz, how many more harvests before you get yourself a wife? You're growing old."

From the dark places surrounding the threshing floor I watch and wait to do as Naomi directed. She bid me, "Stay out of sight until the men are finished eating and drinking. Pay attention so you will know where Boaz lies down. Uncover his feet and lie down."

I peek in from my hiding place watching as the strong arms of men sift and bag grain for selling and trading. The last bag tied and stacked invites celebration. The men gather to eat and drink and rejoice in the harvested abundance.

Though I trust Naomi and her God, questions poke holes in my faith. "How can I, a foreigner, offer myself to such a good man in hopes he will care for me? What kind of woman would dare show herself at this 'for men only' event?" A chill crawls underneath my tunic and over my perfumed skin; I wrap my shawl more tightly about my shoulders.

"What will Boaz think of me? Oh, but I am certain my mother-in-law would not send me out to do evil." Questions continue to tumble around inside my head.

Men rustle about working places comfortable to settle down to sleep. The last of their jests are mumbled and snickering echoes softly from every corner in response as the drowsiness takes over. Then a hush tucks in around the men as they give in to weary bodies and fall hard into sleep; the heavy breathing gives way to snoring. Lifting my skirt up to avoid the loud whisper of fabric brushing the floor sounding an alarm, I gently cross the threshing floor. I find my way through the darkness to the place I saw Boaz recline.

Easing myself down onto the floor, I lift Boaz's cloak ever so slightly and curl up around his feet. After several minutes pass I feel my muscles melt into the warmth of Boaz. The beating of my heart slows to a sigh; and remembering Naomi's last words, "Boaz will tell you what to do," I give in to sleep.

As the night folds in half my sleep is punctured by a whisper echoing loud against the quiet, "Who are you?" Ah the moment I had spent my afternoon preening for breaks into the darkness; Boaz has awakened to the realization someone else shares his cloak.

"It is I, Ruth, your servant," I whisper. "Cover me with your cloak and make me your wife," I speak with more boldness than I could have imagined."

Boaz's response is gracious and kind; he speaks blessings over me. His words suggest my request for his covering is a greater kindness than anything I had done for Naomi. I do not know how that could be. He anoints me with praise, calling me a "woman of noble character." He is taken aback at my choosing him over someone younger; but he is such a good, gracious and wise man.

"It is true," he speaks softly, "I am a close relative, but there is one who is nearer and has first rights to marry you and redeem the land Naomi is forced to sell. I will take care of this matter first thing in the morning. If your nearest kinsman is not willing to take you to be his wife and protect you, I will be more than happy to. Lie down and go back to sleep; leave everything to me."

Sleep is more difficult to fall into after Boaz's warm, eager reception. I am more aware of the man whose feet emanate warmth under the cloak than when I first placed myself in this vulnerable position. The blush of acceptance steals over me stirring up something I have not felt in a long time; and a seed of longing plants itself in my heart bursting with hope. It seems daylight is dragging its feet in the stars with no concern about my future.

Just before the light of day slips through the fading darkness, I awake and prepare to leave before anyone sees I had spent the night on the threshing floor. He quietly requests I hold out my shawl and he pours a generous amount of grain in it; I will not go home to Naomi empty-handed. Head bent, I look up at the face of Boaz. This is the face of a man who has worn out nearly twice as many days as I have, yet aging had not worn him down. No matter what life had handed out to him, he took from it wisdom and grace. His grace meets me, his servant, with mercy and kindness in a place of need and hopeful dependence. He looks kindness and promise into my eyes. No, I will not go home to Naomi empty-handed; for her the details of her well planned night will nourish hope and give us a future greater than either of us could have imagined. —JJ

"It is I, Ruth, your servant," I whisper. "Cover me with your cloak and make me your wife," I speak with more boldness than I could have imagined."

HER PLACE IN GOD'S STORY

In Ruth 1:16-17 we are given a glimpse of an intimate moment between two women on a dirt path, a seemingly insignificant decisive moment. Naomi urges Ruth to turn back and Ruth pleads to go forward into a foreign land to serve the one true God. A bigger picture than either of them could have imagined hangs on these two verses. Ruth, a name that sounds like friendship in the Hebrew language, expressed intense loyalty and attachment when she chose to go back to Judah with her mother-in-law. Ruth's decision served Naomi well, but God's plan for Ruth served all of us well.

Only two books of the Bible were named after women: Ruth and Esther. Ruth was a despised foreigner from a culture steeped in paganism, and yet God chose to highlight her story of redemption.

Ruth was raised in Moab where the people blatantly served false gods through grotesque rituals; yet Ruth had developed into a woman of character. We do not know what Ruth was like before Naomi came into her life, but Ruth's selfless devotion towards Naomi gives us some indication of her mother-in-law's influence.

A woman with a servant's heart is a good descriptor of Ruth; she is the woman who followed and fed her mother-in-law. Ruth was the epitome of love and loyalty. Verse 16 of chapter 1 is one of the most widely quoted verses at weddings. Ruth was committed to leave behind all she knew, including her family, to follow Naomi and her God.

Ruth an unknown woman, became the great grandmother of King David. This places Ruth in the genealogy of Jesus, our Redeemer once and for all. Ruth is one of four women listed in the genealogy of our Savior. What seemed an unimportant choice on a dirt road was background in the beautiful story of Jesus, the One perfect sacrifice for all sin.

THE STORY FINDS ITS PLACE IN ME

1. What parts of the Ruth's story find their place in you?

2. God in His sovereignty used Naomi's risky idea to help Ruth get a husband, providing for the needs of both widows. What surprising things has God done to meet a need in your life? Did any of these experiences require you to first do something that may evoke questions about your motives, or your sanity?

3. Write out your story of redemption. How were you first compelled to follow Jesus?

4. Naomi had such a profound influence on Ruth's faith in God her daughter-in-law was willing to leave all she knew and submit herself to the uncomfortable position of rejection in a foreign land. Describe a time when your influence gave someone the courage to step out in faith no matter the cost.

5. These two women had no idea the significance of Ruth's decision made on a dirt road to Bethlehem. This beautiful picture of love and redemption reflects the creative hand of the sovereign God. It is His eternal painting and we've been placed right in the middle of it. Write about a seemingly small decision you've made, yet it opened up into a journey far more significant than you could have imagined.

NOTES

ESTHER

THE ORDAINED • KEY SCRIPTURE PASSAGE: Esther 5:1-8; 7

HER CONTEXT

Purim is a Jewish holiday that is still widely celebrated by Jews. This holiday is celebrated with a public reading of the book of Esther. It is a holiday focused on thanking God for the deliverance and safety of the Jewish people.

Scholars believe the book of Esther to be an imaginative act of narration rather than an accurate historical record. It is set in the Persian Empire during the latter part of the fifth century BC. During this period, the Jews have been exiled from their homeland; Esther and Mordecai are residents of Susa, one of the four capitals of the Persian Empire at the time. Esther is born with little power: she is a woman, she is an orphan, she is a Jew. This lack of social capital is precisely why she functions so well in this story as a model for the Jewish people—also marginalized and powerless.

HER STORY

Esther traced the subtle lines of makeup on her face. Though she had not been queen for long, it was difficult for her to remember the Jewish orphan girl hidden underneath the face paint, the lavish gowns, the jewelry. Certainly she was beautiful, even without the fine clothes and adornments. It was her beauty that had won her this position, she was sure. Plucked from some four hundred beautiful virgins, potential queens, all assembled for the pleasure and use of His Majesty, King Xerxes. She noticed the admiration in the eyes of the young maid next to her as the girl readied to line Esther's eyes with black kohl.

Her stomach turned. This banquet, though it was just one of a whole litany of them, was perhaps the most important banquet of her lifetime. She'd be asking Xerxes to save her people, and—she doesn't know what is more terrifying—she'd be admitting her heritage: she is a Jew. A Jew in the Persian court.

How did I get here? she asked herself for the hundredth time. Oh God, how did I get here?

But God didn't answer. The only sound in the room was the slow and concentrated breathing of her attendant as she massaged the white lead paint into Esther's skin, giving it a pleasing, if rather inhuman, glow.

Esther wanted to believe Mordecai, that God was grooming her for an important purpose. "For just such a time as this," he'd said. Mordecai was the closest thing to a father she'd known, and he was a man of God. She'd long trusted him to guide her, to help her do what was right in the eyes of the Lord. He'd helped her become queen. He'd helped her gain the King's trust after exposing a plot that two of the king's own servants had hatched against him. He was the person she trusted most in the world. But perhaps Mordecai was wrong this time.

Up to this point, Esther had held little power. She had gotten used to seeing herself as a pawn, had never even thought to aspire to anything more. She was, after all, an orphan, a woman, a Jew. There was little she could do to escape this lot. She'd been shuffled this way and that by men more powerful than herself all her life—adopted and instructed by Modecai, given to the harem to become a concubine of the king. All the prayer and fasting these past days had done little for Esther's confidence; God was silent. Far away. Why would Xerxes listen to anything she might say to him? Her people were doomed.

She tried rehearsing the little speech she'd prepared, the request that could cost her her life: "If I have won your favor, O king, and if it pleases the king, let my life be given me—that is my petition—and the lives of my people—that is my request. For we have been sold, I and my people, to be destroyed, to be killed, and to be annihilated . . ."

Even as she spoke the words under her breath, her heart broke with fear. Xerxes wasn't necessarily known for his compassion and level-headedness. Yes, he loved Esther, but he loved himself more. The only reason she had the crown at all was because Xerxes, in a fit of anger, had deposed the former queen, Vashti, for refusing to appear before him and the men at court. He'd wanted her to come in nothing but her crown, according to the gossip around the castle. Those were the whispers, but Esther knew they were probably true. Where Vashti was now is a mystery. Probably, she was dead. Nevertheless, Esther could not think of Vashti now. Now, there was a decree that all Jews throughout Susa be destroyed. Now, she was the only one who might seek to change the king's mind. Now, she must prepare to feast with King Xerxes and Haman, the wicked man behind the edict.

Oh, God of Abraham, Isaac, and Jacob. Where are you? Why do you hide yourself from your servant?

The maid, finished with Esther's face, nodded slightly at her work.

It is time, Esther thought to herself. The attendant departed, leaving Queen Esther alone in her quarters.

She stood to her full height, layers of fabric from her gown rustling with even this small movement. Her hair shone in tiered ringlets under her crown. Her eyes, edged in vibrant greens and dark blacks, were piercing and deep. The lace and raw silk of her gown were more decadent than anything she had ever touched before coming queen. She was stunning. But her slightly quivering lip betrayed her. Certainly God did not see her now, so assimilated into this pagan culture, the perfect picture of a Gentile queen.

Surely He was as hidden as she was under these layers of Persian adornments, layers that she felt hang on her like weights around her neck.

The thought jarred her, and her breath caught in her throat. Almost as if she was outside of herself, she rushed to the water basin, splashing her face maniacally with the cool water. It ran down her neck, into the bosom of her dress. The bowl muddied. She saw the vibrant green shadow from her eyes, the red stain from her lips, and the dark black from her eyes and brows streak down her skin in rivulets. The shimmering makeup swirled together in the water, each distinct color blending into the rest, into nothing but dirty water. The smell of the myrrh and the saffron assaulted her. She stared at her naked face, still Esther.

It was herself as she had always known herself.

Esther's attendant entered the room, startled at the sight of the queen's dripping face. She ran toward her. "Your Majesty—" she started. But Esther interrupted her.

"I just had to see," she said, still staring at her reflection. "I just had to see. Let's start again." The girl went to find a dry towel.

Esther lowered herself back down into her chair. Her lip no longer quivered.
—KS

"Up to this point, Esther had held little power. She had gotten used to seeing herself as a pawn, had never even thought to aspire to anything more. She was, after all, an orphan, a woman, a Jew."

HER PLACE IN GOD'S STORY

Esther's place in the story of God is an important one. Her name means "I will hide" in Hebrew, and when her story begins, Esther is literally hiding, keeping her Jewish identity a secret from the rest of society. It is not until a threat against her people is leveled, when Haman plots to kill and destroy every Jew in the land—that Esther decides to tell the king her true heritage. This courageous act is also a dangerous one; Esther is both coming clean as a Jew and going to the king of her own volition, unbidden. Her attitude here is brave and admirable, a far cry from the orphan girl we meet at the beginning of the story: "After [three days of fasting], I will go to the king, though it is against the law; and if I perish, I perish" (4:16).

Although Esther is unaware of it, the night before she makes her request before the king, Xerxes can't sleep. He remembers Mordecai, the Jewish man who saved him from an assassination plot some time before. When he finds that Mordecai was never properly honored for this deed, the king instructs Haman to figure out the best reward for a "man the king wishes to honor." In a humorous turn of events, Haman is at once plotting Mordecai's death and (unwittingly) Mordecai's reward (Esther 6). The Book of Esther is the only book in the Bible in which God is not mentioned explicitly, yet the author, through a series of overwhelmingly overt coincidences like these, makes it clear that God is at work in the story.

When Esther finally makes her request of the king in chapter 7, it is clear that he will accept it. Haman is sentenced to the very death he had plotted for Mordecai, the Jews are saved, and Mordecai is exalted to a higher position of authority. In addition, the law is changed to allow Jews to defend themselves, and the enemies of the Jews are slain in two important battles.

Although the book of Esther receives much criticism for its failure to mention God, it is easy to see God's hand in the events of Esther's life. In much the same way as Joseph rises to power, the Jewish characters in this story face overwhelming odds and still succeed. God hides in the details, delivering his people as He has always promised. In Esther's story, we see glimpses of God's faithfulness, even in the midst of ambiguity and lack of clear direction. She is not only a model for the oppressed and marginalized Jews, but also for twenty-first century Christians who are trapped in unfair or hostile circumstances, who struggle to hear God when He appears to be silent.

THE STORY FINDS ITS PLACE IN ME

1. What parts of Esther's story find their place in you?

2. Have you experienced times in your life when God seems "hidden?" How have you approached these times?

3. Esther is a diaspora narrative, meaning that the Jews are in exile, outside and away from their homeland.

   Think about how Esther and Mordecai navigate this reality. What can you learn from this for times in your life when you are either literally or figuratively outside and away from your comfort zone?

4. God works through a series of human actions and divine providence in Esther's story to bring the Jews, His chosen people, to deliverance. Have you experienced circumstances in which God has worked in one or both of these ways?

5. When Mordecai petitions Esther to go to the king with her concerns for her people, he says, "Who knows? Perhaps you have come to royal dignity for just such a time as this" (4:14). Why do you think he suggests it?

NOTES

RAHAB

THE PROTECTOR • KEY SCRIPTURE PASSAGE: Joshua 2

HER CONTEXT

For most of us, the first thing to come to mind about Canaan, is that it became the promised Land for Israel. Named after Noah's grandson, it was the home to several Semitic groups, such as the Ammonites, Amorites, Moabites, Phoenicians, Ugaritics and Edomites. In Genesis it also earned God's curse for perpetual slavery because of Ham's inappropriate response to his father, Noah's, inebriated state at one time. Although, some may argue about the relevance and staying power of the said curse, Canaan's long ensuing history with Israel would remain one of conquer or be conquered.

Yet before Canaan became the land filled with milk and honey it was more popularly known for its murex shellfish. Kingdoms all over the ancient world would pay for this sea urchin, which created a deep purple dye that was used for the robes of rulers as far as Egypt.

> "Canaan adhered to an agricultural religion and fertility motifs were a common sight."

In fact, the name Canaan was biblically equated with, "trader" or "merchant." However, as much as this trade was growing, the real staple for Canaan was agriculture. Growing crops and farming was still very much the customary employment and in the lush and lean environment that Rahab grew up in, it would have been vital.

Canaan adhered to an agricultural religion and fertility motifs were a common sight. Rahab would have been accustomed to Ashtoreth poles on display, much like shrines in other countries. Perhaps she would even have known of the temples where farmers went to sleep with sacred prostitutes to evoke the gods, Asherah and Ashtoreth in an attempt to yield more crops.

Although historians contest whether this really was a Canaanite religious tradition, others have tried to draw parallels with Rahab's own prostitution and the religious backdrop she was living in. Yet perhaps her profession says more about the limited options available to women, outside of the more expected household roles.

Rahab lived at a time of uncertainty. Other Canaanite kings had been displaced, Egypt had lost a staggering number of slaves and the same Israelite group that was core in those events was now moving towards Jericho's walled city.

HER STORY

I am the first to wake. I can smell the cinder and ash before it has even come, the way others taste iron in the air before rain.

"Will they come? They won't forget us, will they?" The anxious questioning of my family has not stopped since we shut ourselves in the house. I turn to look at my youngest sister,the one who looks the most like me. Our skin is as brown as shelled almonds, our eyes as green as our mother's; the Onan family eyes. Our father's eyes are milky with blindness; thankfully none of us got his eyes. Lastly, we have the same thick, dark curly hair, which turns copper in the summer and black in the winter.

My parents and siblings, their spouses and children, cousins who we barely share blood with- they're all here, crammed onto every inch of rug. They didn't hesitate to come once the word spread of the Israelites moving and coming closer.

"They made me a vow. They'll come." I tell her.

* * *

There are disadvantages to living in a wall. Whatever your neighbor ate for supper will be on your skin and in your hair by the morning and their tendency to crane their necks and peek into your walls is made only too easy by how close we all are.

I close the thin, sheer curtains and light another block of beeswax. The oils in the room have heated and uncurl around the space.

I untangle my hair and check that the black has not smudged around my eyes, pinch my cheeks and bite my lips until they're red. When I hear the knock, I still myself from deep on the inside then answer.

From the way they are dressed and the way they speak my tongue, I know the two men at my door are not from here.

"Please, please, my friend is hurt," one man says, trying and failing to hold up the other whose whole left side seems to be grazed and bleeding.

Doors up and down are already opening. Windows are cracking ajar.

"Please," he says again. This time I see the sweat drop off him.

I nod and he lays his friend on a sheet I put down. I work quickly and quietly. They whisper to each other in another language and I hear the name, 'Joshua.'

"Chew this, it will help with the pain," I say putting fresh clary sage in the wounded man's hand.

He looks at me suspiciously.

"If I wanted to kill you, would I have wasted all that time fixing you?" I ask standing up straight.

"Tell us, are you Rahab?" The friend asks.

"Shouldn't it be you making introductions?"

"Of course. I am Nahem and he is Salmon and we . . ."

"Came to see how your people could break our walls," I finish for him. I sit on cushions and watch them. The smell of ash and smoke clings to them as much as the heat of fire does.

"You know of us?" stutters Salmon, wincing with every word.

"We've heard the stories of what your God did to Egypt. How he buried them in the sea, but not before holding it open for you to get out." I say recalling what had been murmured and whispered through all these walls. It was always just a whisper though. The King did not like to be reminded there was power greater than his.

"We know what you did to Og and Sihon. I know that this land will all be yours." I say it softly, but it's loud in my head.

"But you're so calm about it all," says Salmon, gingerly moving his arm.

I smile, more to myself. "Some things have been told long before us."

The low whistle of a horn interrupts us, reaching right into the room.

"The guard," I say standing up quickly.

"We'll leave. Thank you for your kindness," says Salmon, using Nahem's arm to haul himself up.

"You'll be dead before you reach the eastern quarters," I say frankly. Salmon is sweating even more than Nahem.

"We cannot stay," Nahem insists.

"I will hide you, follow me," I hear myself reply

"Thank you, Rahab." He says my name in such a strange way. It's as if the 'r' has been given a new life. The horn sounds again. It is closer this time.

"Come this way," I say and lead them through a small doorway to steps. The stairs stop under a trap door and I carefully ease it open.

The air is thick with summer and tumeric. Nadia must be making her pot of lamb. The stars hang low over us and give more light than the torches or even the moon.

"Here," I usher them. I hold back bundles of drying hay and show them where to lie down.

I give them a curt nod, my finger to my lips and head back downstairs. I hide the herbs and pause by some incense allowing its clouds to swallow me whole.

Then I open my eyes, smile boldly and hold my door open as the guards' feet step closer.

* * *

When I return, they have managed to slow and deepen their breathing so well, I'm not sure they're alive.

"It's safe now," I tell them, holding the hay.

Salmon relaxes, but Nahem moves more slowly, his eyes checking the streets below.

"You've saved our lives. How could we ever thank you," starts Salmon. I watch them and wrestle with the idea growing in my head. I think of my family and I think of my neighbors. I think of the children who play between the market stalls and the men who lie in my bed and cry their apologies. I think of my father's eyes that have never seen what I have become, but whose every bone knows it anyway. And I think of the fire, burning these walls and leaving ash.

"Get my family out before you take this city and I will get you out of here to-night."

"What?" asks Nahem.

"The guards will be back and this time there will be more and they will search every house in these walls. But if you follow what I tell you, they will never find you."

Salmon tilts his head back, his eyes fixed on me. His eyes are gray, an unusual color.

"Your family," he echoes.

"Yes," I answer, ignoring the faces of all the many others who don't share my blood.

"Then tell them, before the first wall falls, they must be inside your house. All of your kin must be here and you must keep this hanging outside of your window," he says reaching into a pouch and pulling out a ball of blood red rope.

"We will be ready," I say taking the rope.

"And now us?" asks Nahem standing up.

"Take the western path. Follow the stench towards the waste and escape to the hill country. Once you get there, hide for three days. The men will search that far for you, but they'll turn back eventually and then you can go on."

"Thank you, Rahab," Salmon says again. "We swear to get your people out."

"You'll not betray us?" asks Nahem.

I look at him sadly and feel the fire coming off him the strongest. "Tell Joshua, Jericho's time has come and gone, our land is no more, but please, have mercy as you conquer."

They slip away so quietly even cats would be impressed and then I am alone on the roof watching as more torches are lit and more horns start to blow. —EL

"I watch them and wrestle with the idea growing in my head. I think of my family and I think of my neighbors. I think of the children who play between the market stalls . . ."

HER PLACE IN GOD'S STORY

Unlike so many other women of her day, quite a bit has been written about Rahab. She is the first Gentile woman mentioned by name in Jesus' lineage in Matthew. James hails her actions of hiding the two Israelite spies as the epitome of faith lived through deeds. And the story of the scarlet rope has created scores of stories and sermons over the years.

The second thing most of us know after Rahab's name, is that she was a prostitute. She would have experienced the social snobbery, outright prejudice, disregard, criticism, and the judgment of so many. However, Rahab does not play the pawn in the story and by the end of her two appearances in Joshua, has managed to settle an arrangement that will save her family and relatives from certain death. Unlike later stories in the New Testament, this prostitute uses her skill and sway for very real mercy and favor. (Josh. 2:12-21, Josh. 6:22-25)

Rahab shows in this short tale that faith can be found in the most unexpected of places. She is not Jewish, she has not had personal experiences with this Yahweh, yet she recalls his most spectacular miracles to the spies and personally heralds Israel's conquest. Furthermore, she makes it quite plain that this God is beyond those worshipped amongst her own people. (Josh. 2:8-11)

This story is another reminder that faith and salvation come to all regardless of ethnicity. As a Canaanite, Rahab would have been brought up in the ways of Baalim and Baalot, Ashtoreth poles and temples, where sexual practices were part of divine religion. Yet, unlike Achan, who broke faith in God and his brethren soon after the conquest (Josh. 7:16-26), Rahab was single-minded in her beliefs of God's abilities.

Not only is Rahab listed as King David's great-grandmother and so Jesus' predecessor, she brings the Gentiles right into the heart of the Jewish people and perhaps acts as a herald of a new time to come.

THE STORY FINDS ITS PLACE IN ME

1. What parts of Rahab's story find their place in you?

2. When have you stood where Rahab did? Where you have been faced with news that completely undoes all you thought you understood about yourself, where you grew up and what you believed in?

3. Rahab defies every stereotype given to her. She does not succumb to people's judgments on her ethnicity, gender, or paid work. Instead she takes action to save the lives of herself and her loved ones. Are there things in your past that you feel hinder you today? How can you rise above them?

4. Despite learning that Israel is seeking to conquer Canaan, Rahab does not retreat to flight mode, instead she uses her courage and wit to rescue those closest to her. Perhaps we can see that love motivated her more than fear. Are you moved to action in crisis? Can you see another purpose in the thick of it all?

5. Rahab chooses to go with Yahweh, in spite of the impending doom he is about to bring to her homeland. She heard the tales and hearsay, yet in him is where she lays her faith. Can you trust God as unabashedly?

DEBORAH

THE VOICE • KEY SCRIPTURE PASSAGE: Judges 4-5

HER CONTEXT

After Joshua, Israel had no centralized leadership. It was a time before a monarchy, "In those days, there was no king in Israel, everyone did what was right in his eyes." (Judg. 21:25) For the most part, this worked. Ancient Jews were dedicated to the Torah. It was not simply religion, but identity and culture. They strove to follow its rules and to be in peace in Canaan.

However, settling into their foreign homes, intermarriage and the consequential adoption of pagan religious practices meant a steady and oft decisively punished fall out would occur.

The judges were those who were there to rescue the people. Through prayer and mediation they would try to discern God's will before making legal and lasting decisions. They were there to remind people to repent and try to restore spiritual order in times when it had gotten lost (Judg. 3: 9-11). Some have suggested the position of judges stemmed from the assistants Moses appointed to help him hear the scores of cases that were brought to him daily (Exod. 18).

We find Deborah ruling Israel for 40 years from 1107 BC. Israel had been under King Jabin of Hazor for 20 years. It was a time described as ruthless oppression and torment. Although there has been some biblical confusion as Joshua is said to be the one who defeated Jabin and razed Hazor to the ground, it has since been tentatively agreed that Deborah's King Jabin may have been a descendant of the earlier king.

Foreign kings before had overrun Israel. Jabin had Sisera, a military commander with over 900 iron chariots. This was also the period of the first iron age between 1200-1000 BC and with it the rise of better honed weapons.

During Deborah's time, communities would have been in villages built on hilltops in mud brick houses on stone foundations that remained under the jurisdiction of larger towns. People would also have lived largely agrarian lives and planted crops like wheat, lentils and chickpeas.

The most glaring fact in this story is that Deborah is the first and only female judge. In a heavily patriarchal society, her rise to such a position speaks volumes of her character, personality, and people's trust in her.

HER STORY

I wake before the sun does, because Samuel Heffez's rooster makes it a point to wake everyone when he sees fit.

The last images of my dreams last night skip in front of me. The picture is dark like cast iron and is as heavy. But it's gone before I can name any part.

The sky outside is shifting from purple to pink and burning wood fills the air. That will be Beth, getting the water to boil. She would have milked the cows already and fed and watered them. I'm still not sure when her day ends and begins.

I turn over and my arms land on the empty space beside me. There is a dent where Lappidoth lay last night. I did not hear him come in and I did not hear him leave.

He will have woken to light the kilns and get their fires burning for the day's pots and dishes he will form with his ever-muddy hands.

I lie back and close my eyes at this blissful morning moment.

"Give it back!" A shrill voice screams.

My eyes are open and waiting.

"No. It's my turn."

Leila and Lisabet are our twin daughters. They came to us late in life. We had little hope we would hold such small treasures in our arms. Many said it was because God had already given us so much in my "gift."

I had spent more tears and we had known many a cold, silent night in those long years. And then, on their own fancy, our daughters arrived. Separated by only three minutes, they filled our quiet solitude with their triumphant noise.

The door opens before my sandals are on and they have tumbled into the room. They fall in and find their feet, still balancing, even without letting go of the doll that's stuck between them. Nowadays I solve disputes both at work and at home.

* * *

The room of peace, as it's called, isn't really much of a room. But there are smooth stone slabs on the ground that keep it cool when there are so many people pressed inside.

They come with papers scrunched in angry palms, bleating goats, distracted teenagers and runaway servants. They come from the moment I sit down in the sturdily made chair, until the sun starts to fall asleep.

Today is no different until a father kneels weeping. It's not for reverence that he is down there, but weakness. I listen as he tells us all about a raid, his family's shame and what will be his daughter's ever-living prison.

"Jabin must pay!" A man yells. He follows it with spit and soon the stone floor is covered.

"May the curses that fell on Pharaoh be on him!" another voice joined in.

"What does the Lord say, Deborah?" a woman asks. I watch her and she's holding a weeping woman who looks like she has gone gray overnight.

I know without asking she is the girl's mother and with the same certainty I see the cast iron darkness of last night again.

"Call for Barak, son of Abinoam. For the Lord has heard his people's cry. He has seen what has become of us and he has mercy." I say and I see both the parents breathe deeply and sink down to the ground.

* * *

Barak is not a very tall man, but he makes up for it with gall and confidence. I don't doubt that is why he was chosen to stand here with these men at the foot of Mount Tabor.

The sun has made his skin even browner and his hair has more salt in it since we last met. There are lines around his eyes and mouth that say everything he won't.

"Are your men ready?" I ask. I can see them, all ten thousand of them. They are divided into battalions. Some are sharpening swords whilst others shape their arrows and tighten bows.

"They are. Whether it be for victory or death," he says solemnly.

"So, you're still not sure?" I eye him closely.

He sighs heavily, it's made difficult by the armor he is wearing.

"As I told you in the room of peace, I say again. The Lord will give you victory. But because you have not fully trusted, you will not receive all the honor. Sisera will be defeated by a woman."

Barak looks at me with raised eyebrows, a playful look on his face.

"At least now I can be sure the Lord will not forsake us," he smiles tightly, nods curtly and stamps down the hill to one of his band of men.

We feel the roll of the chariot's wheels before we even hear or see them. There are so many of them. They come steadily down the hill, their horses moving in a controlled march.

Sisera is positioned at the front. His chariot, the exact same as his men, only he stands taller on it. One hand holds a shield, the other a sword and yet he doesn't fall out.

Barak takes off his helmet and yells something to his soldiers. The words are lost in the deepening drumming of the horses' hooves. He looks up once to where

I stand and raises his sword before turning to run straight into Sisera's line of marching men.

They fight from when the sky is pale and overcast until it deepens and darkens. It's hard to tell what the time is because everything is the same. The screams, the smashing iron, the broken spears, wheels and bones. Everywhere smells like blood, iron on top of iron. But it's the crying that confuses all. There is so much pleading as men beg for more time on this earth.

The sky is pitch charcoal now, the clouds swollen and angry. When they finally burst, I just have enough time to spot Barak cornered but pushing back, when the rain comes.

It is immediate. The horses slip and crush their riders. Sisera's men fall on their own swords. Their armor pulls them deeper in the mud that was the battlefield.

There is a different sound in the air now as the men of Naphtali and Zebulun charge Jabin's army. I see Sisera leave. He has mounted a horse and his tall frame is stooped over low. He looks back and for a moment we see each other and I know he will not die here in the mud. He spurs his horse on and pushes off, but not before I can name what else I have seen in him: dread.

* * *

The tambourines and drums are beaten with such determined care they sound like the heart's thud and the rain that quashed Sisera's threat that day.

Women hold banners and walk in groups singing in harmonies that their mothers and aunts taught them. They sing loudly and they've already created words to chart all that has befallen and been settled.

I hang back because unlike the rest of them I still see Sisera.

Jael had fallen to her knees when Barak and I arrived. She had bathed, I could smell the lilies, but blood can stain quickly and there were still spots of it on her cheeks and fingertips.

She pulled open the tent where he still lay and took off the sheet that hid his broken frame.

The tent peg was staked in his temple and his body was rigid with permanent sleep, but for whatever reason I could still see his last look and knew even as Jael tiptoed to him, that same dread had stalked him into his milk-curd nap.

I touched Jael's thick, curly brown hair as I left and called her blessed. For I may be the one that can dream and prophesy, but it is she that swung a hammer that has changed our whole course.

And now we rejoice, whilst somewhere his mother grieves. The young village girl's parents will bring an offering to the temple and I will hold my daughters, knowing the Lord our God is true. —EL

HER PLACE IN GOD'S STORY

Scripture is rather thin on details about her 40 years of ruling, but the few interactions we see in Judges 4-5, briefly hint at the respect she was given and inspired.

Deborah has the double honor of being both the only female judge and the only judge to be called a prophet. (Judg. 4:4) Deborah trusted in the gift given her and what God had shown her. Prophecy was certainly a gift she shared with her community and especially with Barak when Israel faced 900 iron chariots with much less armed force or manpower.

Perhaps most significant is that her word under that palm tree was the deciding vote in disputes. Furthermore, Barak, an Israelite fighter, who despite a clear prophecy of success, refused to fight without Deborah going along shows just how much confidence her peers had in her.

Although we can only speculate whether she and Lappidoth had their own family, we do know that by the time of her famed song, she was called 'mother of Israel' (Judg. 5:7). Not only does that suggest her seniority in society, but also that she had the kind of personality people could trust to protect them. Perhaps it shows her tireless compassion, devotion and sacrifice to her fellow Israelites? And her ever-swelling love to her "children."

A spectacular thing about Deborah is that she seems genuinely unafraid of war. When Barak pushes back on her prophecy and requests that she go with him she simply agrees and goes with him to Kedesh and on to Mount Tabor. Even though she would not have fought, she would have sang songs to encourage Israel's fighting tribes and reminded them of their win. Maybe it is no coincidence that the name Deborah or Dvora means, "bee." Insects revered for the honey they make in groups and feared for their sting.

"They come with papers scrunched in angry palms, bleating goats, distracted teenagers and runaway servants. They come from the moment I sit down in the sturdily made chair, until the sun starts to fall asleep."

THE STORY FINDS ITS PLACE IN ME

1. What parts of Deborah's story find their place in you?

2. This story happens at a time of heavy oppression under King Jabin. Alongside her community, Deborah would have endured hardships and bad treatment and seen others in difficult circumstances. It would be easy and understandable to feel neglected by the God one has so firmly believed in. Yet as we read her story in scripture we see nothing but confidence in God's plan. How committed are you to believing God?

3. Deborah was truly living as a woman in a man's world. There is no mention about the criticism and challenges she would have experienced, but considering women's prime life objectives were to marry well and have children, especially sons, it's clear she would have faced some resistance. What difficulties have you had to overcome in your sphere of influence?

4. Most of us do not live in the midst of physical war directly, but what things have you been under that have affected your growth? Have fear, manipulation, worry or anxiety been old banes in your life?

5. Deborah's gift of prophecy also shows her to be a great listener to hear God. Have you listened in to what God has tried to share with you in whichever place you find yourself?

NOTES

OTHER STUDIES IN THE NAMED SERIES:

The Unnamed

The Disciples

The Patriarchs

www.iamnamed.com

BEACON HILL PRESS
OF KANSAS CITY